IDIOSYNCRATIC Poetry GUIDE PYRAMID

A GUIDE TO DAILY POETRY CHOICES

RHYMING
PLAGIARISM
NORTON ANTHOLOGY
WALT WHITMAN
PERFORMANCE POETRY
SURREALISM · METAPHOR
WILLIAM CARLOS WILLIAMS
JOHN SKELTON · EZRA POUND

FATS, OILS, AND SWEETS
· USE SPARINGLY

MILK, YOGURT, CHEESE
GROUP
· 2-3 SERVINGS

WILLIAM SHAKESPEARE
JOHN CAGE
WALT WHITMAN
SAPPHO · HUMMING BIRDS
BRUCE CHATWIN
ERNEST SHACKLETON

EMMA GOLDMAN
CATULLUS
GERTRUDE STEIN
SPARROW
BUCKMINSTER FULLER
PAUL GOODMAN

MEAT, POULTRY, FISH
BEANS, EGGS,
NUT GROUP
· 2-3 SERVINGS

VEGETABLE
GROUP
· 2-4 SERVINGS

THINKING · LANDLORDS
PHYSICS · BIRDS · LIGHT
WEATHER · GEORGE PEREC
LEONORA CARRINGTON
ROBERT BYRD · TORTELLINI
GERTRUDE STEIN

EPIGRAM · ALLEGORY
INSULT POEM
OCCASIONAL POEM
OULIPO · PROVENÇAL
PAPPARDELLE · N + SEVEN
BUTTERFLIES · MUSHROOMS

FRUIT GROUP
· 2-4 SERVINGS

EMILY DICKINSON · FIELD GUIDES · DADA · PLAGIARISM
DREAM JOURNALS · BERNADETTE MAYER'S EXPERIMENT LIST
LANGSTON HUGHES · ETYMOLOGICAL DICTIONARY · COLLABORATION
GREEK ANTHOLOGY · PHYLLIS WHEATLEY · DANTE ALIGHIERI
SIR WALTER RALEIGH · RIBOLLITA · BLUE HERONS · POMEGRANATES

BREAD, CEREAL, RICE, PASTA GROUP
· 6 - 11 SERVINGS

BY BERNADETTE MAYER, PHILIP GOOD, MARIE WARSH

Please Add to This List

Teaching Bernadette Mayer's
Sonnets & *Experiments*

TENDER BUTTONS PRESS
New York City
2014

Published by Tender Buttons Press, copyright 2014.
All texts copyright the individual authors.

All rights reserved. No parts of this book may be reproduced in any form without the author's written permission, except for brief quotations in reviews.

"Making Strange" originally published by *Poetry Flash*. "Idiosyncratic Poetry Guide" originally published in *ecopoetics* no. 3. "Blousy Guitar" originally published in *Granta*. Selections from *Journal of Ugly Sites* were originally published in *Drunken Boat*. "Mortal Sonnets" & "Altars Everywhere" originally appeared in *Colorado Review*.

Tender Buttons Press
Lee Ann Brown, Founding Editrix
New York, New York
www.TenderButtonsPress.com

Tender Buttons Logo by Joe Brainard, printed with permission.
Cover art: Christine Shan Shan Hou, *it could be telepathic*, 2014.
Collage on paper.
Cassandra Gillig designed this book and is hot.
Edited by Katy Bohinc.

Cataloguing-in-publication data available from the Library of Congress. 2014952835

ISBN 978-0-927920-08-7

Printed by BookMobile.

Contents

Editor's Note

The idea of "canon" is appalling to Bernadette Mayer—a club she would not enter alone without her students, comrades and contemporaries; she credits this piece of writing, *Experiments*, as "written with her St. Mark's Poetry Project Workshop." This piece of writing which performs in so many directions: as pragmatic muse, as granting of permission, as *Ars Poetica* about not "what is poetry," but literally "what poetry can be"—which says it all about Mayer's Poetics. Mayer's poetics include just about everything (and radically well or better at that), but I'll mention here poetry as communal practice: the poetry of dialogue whose daily place in the wordplay of society means everything to all of us. In *Experiments*, Mayer opens the door to generativity in the most democratic of manners. And how expansive and resonant the conversation! What a terrific symbol of our era!

Here we've included a version of *Experiments* handed out at Mayer's Poetry Project Workshop (previously unpublished), as well as several responses from poets and non-poets alike. Some of the responses were written for this book, others taken from projects or pieces long in conversation with Bernadette's *Experiments* or *Sonnets*. Some are written by readers who are not poets and knew nothing of Bernadette Mayer (my mother, for example) until they were asked to write for this book. We've included, as well, the first review of *Sonnets* by Dawn-Michelle Baude, a piece whose detailed analysis gives great context for any reader of *Sonnets*, and interesting insights into the poetry conversation at the time of first publication by Tender Buttons Press in 1989. We imagine this guide will be helpful to students or teachers of Bernadette Mayer or poetry in general, and hope it serves doubly as artifact for the aficionado. Maybe the first "experiment" is to outline how each response poem relates to Bernadette's list...

Mayer's *Experiments* enact her magnificent oeuvre's sensibilities: the reinvention of the traditional form in *Sonnets*; the expansion of consciousness in her hypnogogic poems, in *Studying Hunger Journals, The Ethics of Sleep* and other works; her original investigations in *Memory*; and etcetera and etcetera, the correlations and broadenings of Mayer's work being endless and endlessly wonderful. Thank you Bernadette for your leadership in teaching us how to be better teachers, as in knowing we learn as much as we teach, that none of us are closed, that all of us are citizens in the land of language and what we say and how far we dream into everything can be reinvented, can be reimagined, can be improved towards a greater peace, a more open field.

Please add to this list.

Katy Bohinc
Star Archestress
Tender Buttons Press

Experiments

by Bernadette Mayer & her St. Mark's
Poetry Project Workshop, circa the
mysterious year of 1988

Pick a word or phrase at random, let mind play freely around
it until a few ideas have come up, then seize on one and
begin to write. Try this with a non-connotative word, like
"so" etc.

Systematically eliminate the use of certain kinds of words or
phrases from a piece of writing: eliminate all adjectives from
a poem of your own, or, take out all words beginning with 's'
in Shakespeare's sonnets.

Rewrite someone else's writing. Experiment with theft and
plagiarism.

Systematically derange the language: write a work consisting
only of prepositional phrases, or, add a gerund to every line
of an already existing work.

Get a group of words, either randomly selected or thought
up, then form these words (only) into a piece of writing—
whatever the words allow. Let them demand their own form,
or, use some words in a predetermined way. Design words.

Eliminate material systematically from a piece of your own
writing until it is 'ultimately' reduced, or, read or write it
backwards, line by line or word by word. Read a novel
backwards.

Using phrases relating to one subject or idea, write about another, pushing metaphor & simile as far as you can, for example, use science terms to write about childhood or philosophic language to describe a shirt.

Take an idea, anything that interests you, or an object, then spend a few days looking & noticing, perhaps making notes on, what comes up about that idea, or, try to create a situation or surrounding where everything that happens is in relation.

Construct a poem as if the words were three-dimensional objects to be handled in space. Print them on large cards or bricks if necessary.

Write as you think, as close as you can come to this, that is, put pen to paper and don't stop. Experiment with writing fast and writing slow.

Attempt tape recorder work. That is, recording without a text, perhaps at specific times.

Make notes on what happens or occurs to you for a limited amount of time, then make something of it in writing.

Get someone to write for you, pretending they are you.

Write in a strict form, or, transform prose into a poetic form.

Write a poem that reflects another poem, as in a mirror.

Read or write a story or myth, then put it aside &, trying to remember it, write it five or ten times at intervals from memory. Or, make a work out of continuously saying, in a column or list, one sentence or line, over & over in different ways, until you get it "right".

Make a pattern of repetitions.

*   *   *

Take an already written work of your own & insert, at random or by choice, a paragraph or section from, for example, a psychology book or a seed catalogue. Then study the possibilities of rearranging this work or rewriting the 'source'.

Experiment with writing in every person & tense every day.

Explore the possibilities of lists, puzzles, riddles, dictionaries, almanacs, etc. Consult the thesaurus where categories for the word 'word' include: word as news, word as message, word as information, word as story, word as order or command, word as vocable, word as instruction, promise, vow, contract.

Write what cannot be written, for example, compose an index.

The possibilities of synesthesia in relation to language & words: the word & the letter as sensations, colors evoked by letters, sensations caused by the sound of a word as apart from its meaning, etc. And the effect of this phenomenon on you, for example, write in the water, on a moving vehicle.

Attempt writing in a state of mind that seems least congenial.

Consider word & letter as forms—the concretistic distortion of a text, a multiplicity of o's or ea's, or a pleasing visual arrangement: "the mill pond of chill doubt."

Do experiments with sensory memory: record all sense images that remain from breakfast, study which senses engage you, escape you.

Write, taking off from visual projections, whether mental or mechanical, without thought to the word in the ordinary sense, no craft.

Make writing experiments over a long period of time, for example plan how much you will write for a particular work each day, perhaps one word or one page.

Write on a piece of paper where something is already printed or written.

Attempt to eliminate all connotation from a piece of writing & vice versa.

Experiment with writing in a group, collaborative work: a group writing individually off of each other's work over a long period of time in the same room; a group contributing to the same work, sentence by sentence or line by line; one writer being fed information & ideas while the other writes; writing, leaving instructions for another writer to fill in what you can't describe; compiling a book or work structured by your own language around the writings of others; or a group working & writing off of each other's dream writing.

Dream work: record dreams daily, experiment with translation or transcription of dream thought, attempt to approach the tense & incongruity appropriate to the dream, work with the dream until a poem or song emerges from it, use the dream as an alert form of the mind's activity or consciousness, consider the dream a problem-solving device, change dream characters into fictional characters, accept dream's language as a gift.

Experiment with every traditional form.

Write poems and proses in which you set yourself to the task of using particular words, chosen at random like the spelling exercises of children: intelligence, amazing, weigh, weight, camel, camel's, foresight, through, threw, never, now, snow, rein, rain.

*   *   *

Write the poem: ways of Making Love. List them.

Diagram a sentence in the old-fashioned way. If you dont know how, I'll be happy to show you; if you do know how, try a really long sentence, for instance from Melville.

Turn a list of objects that have something to do with a person who has died into a poem or poem form, in homage to that person.

Write the same poem over and over again, in different forms, until you are weary. Another experiment: Set yourself the task of writing for four hours at a time, perhaps once, twice or seven times a week. Don't stop until hunger and/or fatigue take over. At the very least, always set aside a four-hour period once a month in which to write.

* * *

Attempt as a writer to win the Nobel Prize in Science by finding out how thought becomes language, or does not.

Take a traditional text like the pledge of allegiance to the flag. For every noun, replace it with one that is seventh or ninth down from the original one in the dictionary, for instance the word "honesty" would be replaced by "honey dew melon." Investigate what happens; different dictionaries will produce different results.

Attempt to write a poem or series of poems that will change the world. Does everything written or dreamed of do this?

Write occasional poems for weddings, for rivers, for birthdays, for other poets' beauty, for movie stars maybe, for the anniversaries of all kinds of loving meetings, for births, for moments of knowledge, for deaths.

Structure a poem or prose writing according to city streets, miles, walks, drives. For example: Take a fourteen-block walk, writing one line per block to create a sonnet; choose a city street familiar to you, walk it, make notes and use them to create a work; take a long walk with a group of writers, observe, make notes and create works, then compare them; take a long walk or drive—write one line or sentence per mile. Variations on this.

The uses of journals. Keep a journal that is restricted to one set of ideas, for instance, a food or dream journal, a journal that is only written in when it is raining, a journal of ideas about writing, a weather journal. Remember that journals do not have to involve "good" writing—they are to be made use of. Simple one-line entries like "no snow today" can be inspiring later. Have 3 or 4 journals going at once, each with a different purpose. Create a journal that is meant to be shared and commented on by another writer—leave half of each page blank for the comments of the other.

Type out a Shakespeare sonnet or other poem you would like to learn about/imitate double-spaced on a page. Rewrite it in between the lines.

Find the poems you think are the worst poems ever written, either by your own self or other poets. Study them, then write a bad poem.

Choose a subject you would like to write "about." Then attempt to write a piece that absolutely avoids any relationship to that subject. Get someone to grade you.

Write a series of titles for as yet unwritten poems or proses.

Work with a number of objects, moving them around on a field or surface—describe their shifting relationships, resonances, associations. Or, write a series of poems that have only to do with what you see in the place where you most often write. Or, write a poem in each room of your house or apartment. Experiment with doing this in the home you grew up in, if possible.

Write a bestiary (a poem about real and mythical animals).

Write five short expressions of the most adamant anger; make a work out of them.

* * *

Meditate on a word, sound or list of ideas before beginning to write.

Take a book of poetry you love and make a list, going through it poem by poem, of the experiments, innovations, methods, intentions, etc. involved in the creation of the works in the book.

* * *

Write the longest most beautiful sentence you can imagine— make it be a whole page.

Set yourself the task of writing in a way you've never written before.

* * *

What is the value of autobiography?

Attempt to write in a way that's never been written before.

Invent a new form.

Write a "perfect" poem.

Write a work that intersperses love with landlords.

Plan, structure, and write a long work.

*　*　*

What is communicable now? What is more communicable?

What is the poem of the future?

*　*　*

Compose a list of familiar phrases, or phrases that have stayed in your mind for a long time—from songs, from poems, from conversation:

> *What's in a name? That which we call a rose*
> *By any other name would smell as sweet* (Romeo & Juliet)
> *A rose is a rose is rose* (Gertrude Stein)
> *A raisin in the sun* (Langston Hughes)
> *The king was in the counting house*
> *Counting out his money...* (nursery rhyme)
> *I sing the body electric...*
> *These United States...* (Walt Whitman)
> *A thing of beauty is a joy forever* (Keats)
> *(I summon up) remembrance of things past* (WS)
> *As not for whom the bell tolls*

It tolls for thee (Donne)
Look homeward, Angel (Milton)
For fools rush in where angels fear to tread (Pope)
All's well that ends well (WS)
I saw the best minds of my generation destroyed by
madness (Allen Ginsberg)
I think therefore I am (Descartes)
It was the best of times, it was the worst of times... (Dickens)
O brave new world that has such people in it
      (Shakespeare, the Tempest,
        later Huxley)
Odi et amo (I hate and I love) (Catullus)
Water water everywhere
Nor any drop to drink (Coleridge)
Curiouser and curiouser (Alice in Wonderland)

Write what is secret. Then write what is shared. Experiment with writing in two different ways: veiled language, direct language.

Write a soothing novel in twelve short paragraphs.

Write a work that attempts to include the names of all the physical contents of the terrestrial world that you know.

Take a piece of prose writing and turn it into poetic lines. Then, without remembering that you were planning to do this, make a poem of the first and last words of each line to see what happens. For instance, the lines (from Einstein):
   When at the reception
   Of sense-impressions, memory pictures

Emerge this is not yet thinking
And when...
Would become:
When reception
Of pictures
Emerge thinking
And when

And so on. Form the original prose, poetic lines, and first-and-last word poem into three columns on a page. Study their relationships.

* * *

Write a macaronic poem (making use of as many languages as you are conversant with).

Attempt to speak for a day only in questions; write only in questions.

Attempt to become in a state where the mind is flooded with ideas; attempt to keep as many thoughts in mind simultaneously as possible. Then write without looking at the page, typescript or computer screen.

Choose a period of time, perhaps five or nine months. Every day, write a letter that will never be sent to a person who does or does not exist , or to a number of people who do or do not exist. Create a title for each letter and don't send them. Pile them up as a book.

Etymological work. Experiment with investigating the etymologies of all words that interest you, including your own name(s). Approaches to etymologies: Take a work you've already written, preferably something short, look up the etymological meanings of every word in that work including words like "the" and "a." Study the histories of the words used, then rewrite the work on the basis of the etymological information found out. Another approach: Build poems and writings from the etymological families based on the Indo-European language constructs, for instance the BHEL family: bulge, bowl, belly, boulder, billow, ball, balloon; or the OINO family: one, alone, lonely, unique, unite, unison, union; not to speak of one of the GEN families: kin, king, kindergarten, genteel, gender, generous, genius, genital, gingerly, pregnant, cognate, renaissance, and innate!

* * *

In a poem, list what you know.

Address a poem to the reader.

Write household poems–about cooking, shopping, eating and sleeping.

Write dream collaborations in the lune form.

Write poems that only make use of the words included in Basic English.

Attempt to write about jobs and how they affect the writing of poetry.

Write while being read to from science texts.

Trade poems with others and do not consider them your own.

Exercises in style: Write twenty-five or more different versions of one event.

Review the statement: "What is happening to me, allow for lies and exaggerations which I try to avoid, goes into my poems."

Please add to this list.

List of Journal Ideas

Journals of:
    dreams
    food
    finances
    writing ideas
    love
    ideas for architects
    city design ideas
    beautiful and/or ugly sights
    a history of one's own writing life, written daily
    reading/music/art, etc. encountered each day
    rooms
    elaborations on weather
    people one sees—description
    subway, bus, car or other trips (e.g. the same bus trip
        written about every day)
    pleasures and/or pain
    life's everyday machinery: phone, stoves, computers,
        answering machine messages
    round or rectangular things, other shapes
    color
    light
    daily changes, e.g., a journal or one's desk, table, etc.
    the body & its parts
    clocks/time-keeping
    tenant-landlord situations
    telephone calls (taped?)
    skies
    dancers
    mail

sounds
coincidences & connections
times of solitude

Other journal ideas:
Write once a day in minute detail about one thing
Write everyday at the same time, e.g., lunch poems,
waking ideas, etc.
Write minimally: one line or sentence per day
Create a collaborative journal: musical notation and
poetry; two writers alternating days; two writing
about the same subject each day, etc.
Instead of using a book, write on paper and put it up
on the wall (public journal).
& so on....

Responses,
Experiments &
Conversations

Shanna Compton
Poet

UNASSUMING, THE KITCHEN TABLE, PLATE 8

List what you know.
That I've begun in an uncongenial mood,
    a congenital statement.
It's not like an infant's eye color.
You can tell right away.

Clear the table first, or use what's in front of you.
Larval stage, a pile of books
and the obdurate rubbish of household,
mail, coffee in a green bowl, the drill and
all its bits, the leak-prone pen. Decluttering
the table just clutters somewhere else.

Alternatively, look around. How far can you see?
I can feel her eyeing me across
several hundred verses of fictional
ocean. The ocean's infinite, actual,
but she's described it in an odd, flat way.
For one thing, it's too long. Also,
she shouldn't be singing. It doesn't work.

Reduce, you pile of disparate functions!
I can go on ignoring the siren. It isn't difficult.
When she changes songs, I adjust my ears.
I've installed a simple button for this purpose.
I could translate or embellish them,

but I'm not that interested,
and I have to stick to the schedule.

Closely regard the casings. Arrange them by size.
The pupae have passed from one developmental
stage into a group of words that happen in relation,
so we'll have to retrain them as they emerge.
The striations of the tightly packed bodies
reflect light, but not all of the light comes
from the expected angle. It's hard to distinguish
their color: they could be black, or dark green.
Someone has opened the blinds and I smell rain.
I nudge the fattest, glossiest chrysalis.
I'm not supposed to touch them.

Arrange a dozen plates on the table.
The eighth plate illustrates the workings
of the lungs, with regard to how they will inflate
the transparent sacs above her wings.
Expect to see that by the third day.

Notice the similarities & the differences.
The siren sings a refrain now: *Close the book.*
She's cheating. She persists with her tired, plain songs.
They are all laments:
*I've made many more meals
in my lifetime than I have eaten,* she's singing.
And I am not halfway through.
None of her songs are new to me.

Choose one to break.
I think this one will hatch soon.

Brenda Coultas
Poet

LOCAL HISTORY SONNET

My sonnet is an airship made of Henry Hudson's red hair
My drone is shaped like the peg leg of Peter Stuyvesant
And like P.S. It delivers just as well
My airship is the Half Moon rising up in flight
A bouncy castle tethered to the local mall
When I think of flight, skinny balloon poodles whimper
and burst
My sonnet has a sail and navigates the sky
Below a tidal river smokes a white clay pipe and wears a
shoe with a square brass buckle.
A real Dutch gem that weathered the sacking of Kingston
How will I ever conquer the great Wall of Manitou, or
know the tricks of light inside of paintings or in the
shadow puppets of Olana?
Fredrick Church wrings out his brushes with glacier water
Washington Irving pilots the bays of Tivoli in a canoe
carved from bone and bluestone
My cabin flies suspended under a vast balloon
There are things that I cannot control

Dodie Bellamy
Poet

20 Experiments for Bernadette Mayer

1. Write a sonnet for sweethearts.
2. Write a sonnet (or series of sonnets) using only words from the "Contents" pages of Bernadette's *Sonnets*.
3. Turn on the television. Copy down the first line of dialogue you hear. Make that the first line of a poem.
4. Sit in a cafe. Listen to the patrons. Copy down the first stupid thing someone says. Make that the beginning of a love poem.
5. Write a sonnet comprised of 14 questions.
6. Google "Bernadette Mayer Exercise." Make a collage of your results, without mentioning Bernadette's name. Instead, translate your results to the first person. Instead of "Bernadette" write "I"; instead of "Bernadette's" write "my," etc.
7. Answer Bernadette's question: Why are we as human beings so sturdy?
8. Write a poem in which you abdicate reality.
9. Write a poem from the point of view of a disjointed bee.
10. Write a sonnet comprised of 14 conclusions.
11. Write a poem about hemispheric faults and colored octaves.
12. Choose a year from your life and research what was happening in the world that year. Weave your personal memories of that year with cultural and political events that were happening concurrently.

13. Go through a favorite novel and copy out every reference to nature—or every color—or gesture.

14. Choose a hyper male novel—a detective novel or something by Norman Mailer or Jonathan Franzen, etc.—copy out every reference to women. Change the references to the first person, so the women are speaking the lines about themselves.

15. Write a story 26 sentences long. Begin the first sentence with A, the second with B, etc., all the way through to Z.

16. Describe a face in orgasm.

17. Copy out a passage of impenetrable theoretical text. Make it the beginning of a sex poem.

18. Write an anthem to Freud's Dora.

19. Copy down every line in the *Sonnets* in which Bernadette uses the words "cock," "cunt," or "vagina." Make a new poem using those lines.

20. List all the things your left hand does that your right hand doesn't know about.

carole wagner greenwood
Chef, artist

sinners sonnet (salty oat)
for jt

Beat. One pound Butter.
yes, beat 1/2 kg unsalted
                    (we never got this right)
3 cups sugar some brown some white
                    a loaded choice DC or Jozi
2 eggs, one & a two
                    i'm alegretto you're lento tempo
2 cups flour, wheat & rice
                    not double entendre. precise.
6 cups oats (& raisins, maybe not)
                    mix by hand get dirty your sore
                    spot
spoon & chill. rest an hour
                    (why not faster? makes us
                    stronger)
smash & sprinkle baking slow

Jen Hofer
Poet

BERNADETTE EXERCISES

Note: anywhere in these exercises where the word "poem" appears feel free to substitute it with "sonnet" or "prose text" instead. It doesn't matter what form you write—it just matters that you write!

- Forget everything you know about sonnets. Forget everything you know about poems. If you didn't know anything about sonnets or poems to begin with, even better! Write a poem.
- Assume nothing. Remember everything. Write a poem.
- Remember nothing. Assume everything. Write a poem.
- Write a poem inspired by the details of an everyday activity—being in line at the supermarket, waiting for your food in a restaurant, making a withdrawal at the ATM, etc. Try writing while actually doing that everyday activity. Then experiment with writing elsewhere, but thinking back on that activity.
- Make a wish. Express that wish in the form of a poem.
- Write a poem that is entirely populated by objects and/ or people who inhabit your home. Then write a poem that is entirely populated by objects and/or people you have only ever dreamt or imagined, but do not know in "real life."
- Write a poem that describes in minute detail some aspect of the city or town where you grew up, or the city or town where you live now.

- Write a poem that has no gender. Then write a poem that relies heavily on gender.
- Write a choose-your-own adventure poem.
- Write a poem that begins by telling someone why you are annoyed with them.
- Write a poem that centers on the death of a well-known person. Include at least three details from that person's life or work, and at least three words that seem to go with that person's name.
- Go to a street corner you know very well, or one that is entirely unfamiliar to you. While you are there, write a poem that begins with a mention of which street corner you are on.
- Read the entire newspaper all the way through (read the print version!). Write a poem.
- Every day for ten days (or however many days you want) clip at least one article from a magazine or newspaper, or bookmark at least one article online. After your days are up, re-read all the articles you've collected. Write a poem. You might use language you find in the articles.
- Spend the day with an animal. Follow the animal everywhere it goes. Try to get inside its perspective, to experience the world as it does. Write.
- Take notes throughout the day—perhaps every time you have a drink of something, or every time you yawn, or every time you send or receive a text message. Use the notes or don't use the notes—write a poem.
- What is an incident? Write at least five "incident report" poems. Consider defining "incident" in both public and private ways. How does that change your poems?

- Listen to two kinds of "input" at the same time—speech in two different languages, or music plus traffic, or café/bar hubbub plus recordings of the ocean, etc. Write a poem.
- Cook a delicious meal for friends you adore. Make sure to encourage your friends to invite at least one person you've never met before. Have lively conversation far into the night. Before you fall asleep, write a poem.
- Immerse yourself in a person, place, atmosphere or idea. Write a praise poem.
- Ask some questions that cannot be answered. Consider the money you owe to whomever you owe it. Contemplate all the shelters where you have lived, and the color of the sky. Write a poem.
- Write a poem or prose text made entirely of sentences or lines from any of Bernadette Mayer's books.

Sophie Seita
Poet

Rewrite someone else's writing. Maybe someone formidable.
—Bernadette Mayer, "Exercises,"
L=A=N=G=U=A=G=E, 1978

throw a few don't's into the waters of your better drainage,
that indulgent retrograde; a water table is all atmospheric
pressure, so smear it on the covers of books—then remove
all temporals—partial or plenary (for the lapse into form can
be captivity or kindness, and grammar is extra-sacramental
and blind); hold them, startled. choose titles that express
the ultimate speculation of love—this is ridiculous—a
grammar that is entertaining is prone to ridicule—so—
read science like the universe believes nothing, write the
new life, the pleasure of species, free of fears of all animal
dangers, exactly, of private apartments, of artless questions,
of making money. kiss and read like a moth & be prepared to
die—the words' relation to the candle the unconscious the
beyond is a joyous appointment. think what can knowledge
accomplish, then sing babies to sleep, then invite reptilian
dreams by name and clothing, without being specious, for
what is the need-be of our culture's desire, and its cure, in
need, if so, but how, for now and the future, but ask yourself
is the epigram, the neat tail, false, by necessity, such bright
short c'mere, and clarity useless like a discarded envelope,
or maybe coveted because so 'accomplished', there is no
turning no abdication, maybe these inadvertent songs are
the most likely octave, so balanced, an unbelievable string
but available & even honest, now think for the fraction of
a—what—line—prosodic fantasy—what do you wish for

them? headlong and coloured there can be rest in thought, a serious understanding of form, this is not conclusive, what is and can it be for a long time I thought I was answering a problem, could instruct, but how can I tell you who already knows of slanted causes of not exactly standard appellations of the beauty of the unlikely unideal sphere of a sonnet—its sublime lodging. let's talk swim in notes eat bread

Hoa Nguyen
Poet, teacher

BLOUSY GUITAR
Made possible by Bernadette Mayer

Blousy guitar   I don't want to count the beats   Hey Hey
My pen   I have bed hair in the best way   Daughter
of sunlight and air   and I'm glad you were born
on this day or put another way: that you were

born   Let's be super stars   Let's call each other "suckas"
Turn everything into writing   Lord of my Love
and eat new raw oysters with many condiments
to lord & love   to be generally great

The flopping flowers that die in a poem
Summer solstice smacks me in the face   ridiculous
and I dream the different   like a naked sonnet
Your raw throaty laugh submerged under hot noodles

I wrote "valley" when I meant "longing"
Your laugh a river   A trout kind of green

Julie Patton
Poet

ACROSTITCH: A SAMPLER

The first time i met Bernadette
she was a song
And the disc burned all the way thru the 4th grade. 4 tops.
Now that I think about it I recall there was a film called
"Song for Bernadette"
The thing is to find a song with someone's name in it and
make it a special
occasion, like an homage or singing birthday telegram, or
you cld call it an epistle poem. For instance 'Goodnight
Irene" or 'Julie Julie Julie
do you love me'
First an individual should find a song with the desired name
in it. Type up
the lyrics, then begin the surgery, listening to measure,
meaning, and nuance, select some nouns, replace with the
letters of the person's full name, in succession, running
down the page. If you run out of letters just start all over
again, or follow it with their birthday or another word
choice such as the name in another language, or the
meaning of said name.
Imagine you are creating text-art so draw attention to this
act by highlighting letters with a different color, size or
typeface, or by using bold.

Bernadette, B *'s are searching for the kind of* E *that* R *possesses*
N *go on searching their whole* A *thru and never find the* D *that*
E *finds in* T

If no such song exists you can create one or take any song
dedicated to a person
and substitute the name for the person you wish to honor.
The point of this exercise is two-fold: one is to create a
visual graphic (similar to a
sampler). You could say I'm a phoneme freak. I secretly
refer to myself as a
phonemenologist. Second, you have to sing it! This means
you have to learn the
song. And connect to sight as well.
This experiment also stitches the subject of the poem to a
hypothetical (name) lineage, to the person the composer
might have had in mind, as well as to the melody, and the
rest of the song's lyrical body. So it's a love poem in that
sense, a love poem filled with
love letters. It can be an epistle, an epithalamium, or
occasional poem.

Let the song's lyric and music guide you. *Sample* what
feels, sounds, or looks right to your eyes and ears.
Leave some nouns and subtract others. You don't have
to replace every one of the suckers. For instance, *you*
or *I* might expand the sense of phonemic play, repeat
certain letters, retain pronouns *we, she, he, thee, me*, if
you wish to exaggerate *E*, hiss at *H* or *S*, make the rap
more personal, inclusive, funky, jazzy, or sexy. Or bend
meaning and gender. Strike a balance between eye
and ear or choose one over the other. Finally, for extra
punch, regard medieval manuscripts and start the first
letter with a bang.

Kyra Lunenfeld
Student

ASSOCIATION FOR LIVES IN TRANSITION

I.

Denied all necessary pleasures, the foreign object –
blue thread in my knee with a scab closing around
now part of my knee, face of

blue, kneeling, now part of the crust around your knees,
final, his face blue,

the foreign body is deprived of all pleasures:

lie down flat piss in a phone booth a little farther away sit
with a hairless cat in a trash bag in your lap free yourself
from the tyranny of maps free from the tyranny of the trash
bag in your lap free from the map of the garbage bag to sit
on your lap a little more time with the hairless cat lying in
the garbage bag sitting without tyranny a little more time

II.

In my travels I have come upon several secrets
of the personal astronaut; I have had many private problems
my mother has confessed to murder she says I'm going to
die
in a fucking bathtub die fucking but
it's not as bad as all that, there is dignity in

protozoan Roanoke, colonial
Empress Elect of pure bone sorrow

all is dignity in
Roanoke, Protozoan Colony of

pure bone, Empress prefers
pure bone, Empress is I was a

Poor imitation of woman I was:
Silent, unseen.

Sandra Simonds
Poet

EXPERIMENTAL SONNET
for Bernadette Mayer

Rewrite someone else's writing. What I mean is
    systematically derange the language. (Whatever
the words allow). Some three-
    dimensional vow to sound, to the hollows.

But Bernadette, the words don't allow, I'm full of
    sorrow, I'm a cloud of
        Fuck it. Rewrite someone
else's bad, bad sadness,
    someone else's bad, bad joy. But the word's

don't allow. And now
    I'm stuck forever
    deranging sound, deranging
        some specific text, some ridiculous
self-awareness or the deliberate, systemic cloud.

Stacy Szymaszek
Purveyor

FROM JOURNAL OF UGLY SITES

7.6 – 7.20

Carroll Gardens: Zagat and NYC DOHMH grade signs on
tinted plate glass windows//garbage day sludge, bonus for
the smell//these common large-leaved weeds wilted in heat
wave//

garden of faux fleurs

partially deflated dirty white balloon, may be more abject//
yellowing condom that Cass sniffs//not much is really ugly
when I eliminate litter//oh, herbicide in the park 7/5, no
chicken bone hunting today, she feels this is an ugly break
from routine//totally fried Bachelor's Buttons//who has the
courage to pull out their appliances//

I did, "let's never let it get that bad again"

old queer's spandexed package perched on the neighboring
bike seat turns me into a rubbernecker, or is it his yellow
tube socks//sugar, goodbye, shriveled organic produce,
condiment shelf goo// disembodied hair//smell of Murphy's
Oil Soap, reminds me of when I had a house, the realty is
what's ugly//Cass likes to pee through the sidewalk grates,
look down to see thick covering of absorbent cigarette
butts//neighbors to ghost properties Preschool of America
and Wonderland Kid Spa//children in the park gather round

Cass, I think "Suddenly Last Summer"//

toe nail fungus of a shoeless man//the same shoeless
man sitting where people have to step over his foot

American Apparel//movie being shot outside my gym//Marco
Polo//coffee grinding controversy, straight to the authorities
some kind of fear of intimacy//looking at the photos you'd
think only heterosexual couples make forever families for
pets//Cass intrigued by growling dogs//2nd time I've stormed
away from the Union deli//new shop where I buy a tank top
despite being under surveillance for being a dyke pay with a
50//elderly woman with cane lapping us again

East Village: cartoon M&M's© key chains hanging from
an ATM sign//plastic waste from 9 people devouring take-
out sushi//it's a mural of a purple tree with a long green
nose and eyeballs//hoard of women at 16 Handles//choir
singing the national anthem, panic, get out so fast zip drive
somehow slips out my silky pocket, GONE despite search
through cobblestones//the e. vill. seems ugly today despite
some attractive people, like Lucy who I remember as a kid in
Milwaukee, then PP intern, now on her way to Iowa – she's
in post work-out euphoria so missed my mild effort to greet–
2nd & 5thish- good luck Lucy!//M-F my own personal hero
tour dead or alive//unsolved murder site where I saw a baby
pig head//fight with Ukrainian Home waitress, standing up
for my committee, we will not be back//horse shit smell, not
the smell but its daily presence//

it's a sauna in here, dancer
sweat, like entering
humanity's glands

Jimmy's whistle and barge maneuver//panic that I forgot the
key so typical but then I find it so typical//soggy almonds
pungent chicken renovations apparently just cosmetic never
going to the Met for lunch again//just green juice now
pulverized by a Polish woman I've been making small talk
with for seven years but when she's off the guys skimp on
the ginger-recent price increase makes it not the best deal
in the village//first I thought everyone was Catholic, then I
thought everyone was responsible//

fuck you and the hummer you rode him over on

revisit train etiquette 1)do not hold the pole with your ass
cheeks 2)I get not wanting to lose your real estate but move
away from the entrance to let me in 3) if you closed your legs
a whole family could sit down//

"east village frozen yogurt scene"//The 13th Step, at least it
was feasible to go to the Telephone Bar//hummer just parked
there like a flaunt

Linda Kozloff-Turner
Poet

FLIGHT M #17 (TO 80 CHILDREN)
A MISTAKE

Wide eyed looking through a window, blue sky
Nestled in the warm breast of her mother
Dozing off to sleep next to her brother
Waiting patiently, planes rise above earth

Sparkling rays of sun spilling down, midday
Tulips waving, cheery, full lips kissing
From this day, it is you, I am missing
Childish splendor, sweet face reaching upward

Blinded by dark, desolate, soulless rage
Thoughtless, sad, angry men marching on
Hollow mechancs, triggers, hands upon
Ground to air missile, explodes, shattered hearts

Raining debris gently lands her rag doll
Any reason for this? Not one, not at all.

Maureen Thorson
Lawyer

EXPERIMENTS AFTER READING BERNADETTE MAYER'S *SONNETS*

- Make a playlist of love ballads from the 1980s. Free write to them while imagining you have artfully bleached and enormous hair.
- Write a poem that is all questions. Write a poem that is full of stock phrases.
- Use a word you wouldn't say to your mom. Doesn't have to be "offensive," though it could be. But a word you could never imagine coming up in conversation with your mom.
- Grow from the mundane out into the fantastical.
- Write a poem that addresses "love." A poem to Love.

Lee Ann Brown
Poet

MORTAL SONNET
for Madeline Gins

Upper limit abstract   Lower limit journal
The problem with dying is that it's really unimaginable

Getting into those corners living is round
Outliving our fears

I can't go on, I'll go on—Philosophical
Unrecorded every second the sonnet

Is not written it changes codes
For better or worse the monied hearse

Lower limit intertextual
Upper limit untouchable

Health is merely the slowest possible rate at which one can
    die
You prefer an able destiny: playfully sliding, making dying
    illegal

Where is Arakawa? I asked Madeline (not knowing)
Eyes surprised: "Near. He is very near"

ALTARS EVERYWHERE
for Amiri Baraka

Amongst the living, man with head held high
Walking across the Wall Street area Afro a.m.
New York—Amiri's gone / he's in the *Times*
the net the culture the hearts of his families
Invented extended even when the little altars
Are washed away he's in dreamtime village
Pitbull Newark Kennedys but without the
Money he said he sang he asked rhetorically
Passionately broke up his "loku" with song—
Was like 2 hours late for a reading but everybody
Stayed—I dreamed again of being inside the family
Of man—birthday specifics and religious questions
James Deas dies the same day—January 9 moon
In Taurus Charlotte North Carolina so long kind men

Jennifer Karmin
Utopographer

3:15 AM
East Nassau, NY
in the home of Bernadette Mayer
August 2009

we all get it sound and cricket sounds sleep sounds hard
to keep eyes open bernadette walks at night is this a poem
how many poems in this house of poems drawer opens what
happens at 3:15 am walk walk not all pens are good for writing
in bed bernadette knocks i yell i'm awake the shock of the
sound of my voice what were you just thinking about in the
dream world the commitment to a project bernadette says oh
shit i don't hear the typewriter yet the typewriter gets turned
on why do we write about what we describe perceive in the
world how long will she type how long will my pen survive
crickets and typing pound the functional part of my brain
wants to make lists of things to do or record the first day
with bernadette all of the stories she has shared the hannah
weiner spider with 7 legs who wants to crawl on me sleep
wants to come the typing typewriter reminds me of being a
child and hearing my mom type the light of a cigarette space
space cough cough typing and handwriting both leave a mark
on the page appreciation thanks for moments of life what
else to write about at 3 am how long does she write for sleep
typewriter how does her brain work why doesn't my brain
work both leave a mark yeah i hear bernadette say the poem
repeats i want to put our brains together for this moment of
time ding goes the typewriter i remember teaching myself
how to type as a junior high student getting books out yes

says bernadette i want to remember yes to keep this voice in my head for the future do these poems get revised things to use to catch a 7 legged spider a strainer is a colander and a plastic bag i don't usually write poems in bed bernadette asks why thrive to grow to succeed to do well to have the pieces to be in a space for 10 years she belongs what are middle of the night poems ding pound the paper i'm sleepy ding what does bernadette write bernadette writes a poem next door yeah i hear how to begin a poem how to end a poem she doesn't give up why to write a poem based on process vs inspiration will she go to bed her laugh cackle HA! a million approximately a million ding a car passing i'm ready

3:15 am
East Nassau, NY
in the home of Bernadette Mayer
August 2010

i try to wake up bernadette will she get up i start writing the house breathes air wind a mosquito bite on my toe paper in every house i think bernadette is awake light or darkness a pen works what comes of head to hand you are a paper clip you are a blanket you are the wind you are a book you are a light you are awake you are asleep blue is asleep blue is awake i prefer to write in blue ink over black ink but i don't know why turn the typewriter on turn her on turn into someone new the news today what can i remember a three year old girl is a hero she goes to the fire station and tells the firemen that her father can't wake up people in nyc protest over a new mosque to be built near ground zero credit card companies need to change their rules one man was driving

around with a loaded shot gun and got arrested and had
to go to jail there was a big fire somewhere the weather is
windy and rainy the local news is different from the national
news oh well i wish i could enjoy katie couric on tv the first
female news anchor on prime time on a major network i
wish i could enjoy the new alice in wonderland movie but
it's too patriarchal she must slay the jabberwocky with a big
phallic sword master and conquer empower one woman over
another then wake up to become a venture capitalist funded
by the old lord's money the caterpillar keeps asking her are
you alice i wonder also is she alice who would have alice
become a story is a myth we all want to believe metaphoric
language of logic bernadette said that western logic has
brought us backwards was aristotle an asshole linear logic is
not really a poetic form i saw a picture of nietzsche's typing
ball on an ipod the typing ball looks like a brain with keys to
push it looks something like what burroughs would enjoy he
believed women are insects bugs butterflies maybe too how
about spiders like the ones that surround bernadette's desk
webs web artist spider sanctuary she's a real organic writer
she's a real orgasmic writer she's a real organized writer she's
a real organ writer she's a real or writer she's a real an she is
a typewriter she is a spider she is a butterfly she is a fly she
is a flower she is a tree she is a picnic table she is a door she
is a bed she is a suitcase she is a curtain she is an ipod she
is a car she is a bank account she is a mosquito she is a pen
she is a notebook she is a paper shredder she is tired i am
tired i will change my position i will lay down and write the
difference between sitting up ideas and laying down ideas
the wind continues to blow the pen continues to write the
poet continues to type light might kite bite site right tight
fight fright flight uptight night goodnight

Jan Bohinc
Social Worker

WHAT WOULD THAT BE?

Bathtube / Lost Vegas / Vinyarn / Kaleidescone
Corrograter / Apostorophize / Productivision
Vacatathrill / Armadillion / Pappillawn
Drawma / Skillette / Forensick / Refractstory
Entertrained / Purchasethon / Ferris World
Lily pack / Saddlebadges / Operating systumble
Hysterectrophy / Cerumbrella / Aquariatlas
Apartmomento / Memorabile / Juxta positron
Springtide / Fleur de lies / Festerday
Bow tile / George Double You / Sysaphysician
Armadillion / Lincoln Funnel / Cest la brie

Laynie Browne
Poet

SONNET EXPERIMENTS LINKED TO BERNADETTE MAYER'S *SONNETS*

1. Dear poet, You are the ultimate lover. Prove your love, your poem. If "Love is a babe" (6) where is it born? Born amid textual touch? Write the poem in which love is newly known, torn, rubbed happily bare. Write the poem in which eros brings a gift with an unknown name. Write the poem which directs the gaze of the reader to a "jewel" of "attention" and to some startling intimate infancy.

2. In Mayer's sonnet beginning

   A thousand apples might you put in your theories
   But you are gone from the benefit of my love

   (10)

   Be a poet in furious love sundered. Write a sonnet which threatens the beloved to remove one's love. What will you take out of the poem? What will you leave in the poem? Write a poem removing apples from theories, including insults and profanities. Consider, what is the non-existent dinner, the absent feast in the absence of love? Are you hungry or stingy? What do you swear and where will you flee?

3. What words would you use to say to your beloved: "You jerk you didn't call me up" (17). Consider technology and also telepathy. Write a lament of absence in which the reader has a choice to "make love" or "die." This isn't a threat, just a textual choice. Here's your chance to describe the trouble with "bourgeois

boys" and "ancestral comforts." What is the most
dangerous cultural soporific of the moment? How will
you "wake up" your lover? In your poem please include
"the middle of the night" and instruct us. What will
satisfy? How to make amends?

4. Write an introduction to your poem, as in "Sonnet:
Twenty Dollars in Hell" (28). Write a poem before
anyone wakes up. Write a "few little songs to be sung
/ before the decimation of the race or love. . " Write a
poem in which poets sink ships or die in or near water.

5. Read "We Eat Out Together" (35) and consider
the geography, color scheme, visual apparatus or
morphology of the heart. Is your heart a "fancy
place" with "a lot of choice among the foods"? If not
"tablecovers to love each other" then what? How will
you "show off poetry's extreme generosity"? In what
vehicle or vehicular company will you ride "home"?

6. Read "Spooky Action from a Distance. . " (57) and
write a poem which breathes deeply, unfulfill's love's
presence. Write a sonnet which is like ". . one of those
/ Displayed wedding cakes on 14th street with a bed
of pink." What will you display in the confectionary
window of your poem? Write a poem that decides it
"might be right to write." Write in "a structure good as
love's or any measure."

7. Read "Sonnet" (70) and write a poem in which "The
arts of death stop by." What do you know about the arts
of death or the death of art? What is "knocking"? What
is there to "conclude"? Where "is love late"? Have you
ever ridden upon the "Old escalators" of "modern art"?
Where did they take you?

8. Read "Sonnet" beginning, "nothing to wake to you

can never" (75) and write a poem including flowers as
characters. If a "sonnet is an offer of a previous peace"
what will you offer? Write a poem in which you
anthropomorphize a day of the week. Write a poem
in which poison and peace may co-exist, or attempt to
co-exist. Who guards the entrance to your poem? Who
guards the entrance to form? What just flew onto your
page? Will you permit it to enter?

9. In her note on *Sonnets*, Mayer writes, "Is the sonnet
    form a form of abdication of reality?" Write a poem
    which makes an argument for or against the abdication
    of reality in poetry. Does objective reality exist? Which
    is less real, the construct of poet or poem? How do you
    define a "real" poet or poem? What is the relationship
    between reality and form? How many forms can you
    take? Where you will take the form of the sonnet in
    your poem?

Laura Henriksen
Sexy werewolf

MORE EXPERIMENTS

Journal of things seen leaned against other things
Journal of places you could have fallen asleep
Journal of Arby's menu items you've wanted
Describe a place without cars, maybe an island
Write the collected letters of Samuel Taylor Coleridge to
his biographer
Write the best and worst house parties of your adolescence
Write the new children's colony
Only meeting minutes
Write a thousand sonnets
Be a skull usurper
Be more of a breakfast person
Record a pop album, be the drummer
Write rococo
Write a chore diary
Write a divine comedy
Write threatening signs for Horrorland Amusement Park
Write a moneymaker
Write a devotional
Write a murder ballad
Let days go by and do nothing about it
Join and break-up a wedding band
Journal of heartbreaks
Over a lifetime – journal of dance crazes
Journal of frog backpacks
Journal of the decline of disco

Number 195

June 1989

Free

FIRST-CLASS MAIL
U.S. POSTAGE
PAID
Berkeley, CA
Permit No. 770

ct
h
St.
003

Review & Literary Calendar

...*aughter Blues*. She received a grant from ...ellowship in Poetry in 1984. She also recently was given a Vesta ...anda Coleman will be reading at Cody's Books on Monday ...e Calendar for details.

Making Strange
☐   DAWN KOLOKITHAS

SONNETS, by Bernadette Mayer. Tender Buttons, New York City. 1989, 87 pages, $5 paper.

THE RUSSIAN FORMALIST, VIKTOR SHKLOVSKY, insisted that one essential component of any poem...

Making Strange
a review of Bernadette Mayer's Sonnets
by Dawn-Michelle Baude

THE RUSSIAN FORMALIST VIKTOR SHKLOVSKY insisted that one essential component of any poem is its *ostranenie* (pronounced "os-tra-nen-ny"), the "making strange" of normal everyday language. In other words, ordering a Greek salad for lunch in a busy Noe Valley café is simply not the same thing as, say, reciting a pantoum or a sonnet. The request for salad—Me Want Salad Now—communicates a straightforward message. The poem, on the other hand, wants primarily to be a poem, the more poem-like the better. It's hard, for example, to mistake a sestina for a food order or an advertisement or a catalogue description. Poems, by their very nature, multiply potential messages, as the opening of Bernadette Mayer's stunning new book, *Sonnets*, illustrates:

> *Love is a babe as you know and when you*
> *Put your startling hand on my cunt or arm or head*
> *Or better both your hands to hold them in my own*
> *I'm awed and we laugh with questions, artless*
> *Of me to speak to ungenerally of thee & thy name*
> *I have no situation and love is the same, you live at home*
> *Come be here my baby and I'll take you elsewhere where*
> *You ain't already been, my richer friend, and there*
> *At the bottom of my sale or theft of myself will you*
> *Bring specific flowers I will not know the names of*
> *As you already have and already will and already do*
> *As you already are with your succinctest cock*
> *All torn and sore like a female masochist that the rhyme*

Of the jewel you pay attention to becomes your baby born

Mayer heeds the postmodern dictum, "make it strange"—an updated version of the modernist admonition, "make it new" (Pound)—at the same time she retains a certain *sonnetness.* She revamps the traditional conventions of the Sonnet form (14 lines, internal divisions, concluding couplet and elaborate rhyme scheme) with risqué diction and radical *ostranenie.* While the quatrains, each organized around a different idea, do not scream out "I'm a four-line unit of intention" they are most assuredly there, subtly embedded. Mayer's sonnet *is* 'strange' in Shklovsky's sense of the term, from the rather meek "come be here my baby" (instead of the predictable "come here be my baby") to the more extreme "there / At the bottom of my sale or theft of myself will you / Bring specific flowers..." This poem introduces the reader to a sonnet sequence where interpretations and readings multiply at an exponential rate, where the ever-popular question— "But what does 'it' mean?"—won't yield a superficial, one-dimensional response.

And yet the book is about something which is dear to most of us. In the "Note" to the book she writes, "Love must be a subject I felt." In *Sonnets* "the poetesses [who] beg forgiveness before your available hardons" are obviously in good company. Like the troubadours encyclopedic fascination with the code of love, or H.D.'s proclamation that great lovers and great artists go hand-in-hand, or even the titillated Catallus's obsession with coy Lesbia, Mayer's interest in love is thoroughly integrated into her poetics, so that she can write with conviction. "*This* [sonnet] proves all who make love tonight are good poets..." (my italics).

That other fabulous sonneteer, William Shakespeare, embraced love as *his* subject as well. Not surprisingly, there are echoes of Shakespeare throughout Mayer's sonnets, including direct quotes like "Love is a babe…" The sequence of poems for "Grace," with lines like "But I can only praise you with this poem," immediately recall Shakespeare's sonnets #17-#23, where, in celebration of the Beloved, he contrasts the permanence of writing with life's ephemera, imparting golem-power to the poem: "So long as men can breathe or eyes can see, / So long lives this and gives life to thee."

Generally speaking, gender can be as ambiguous in Mayer as it is in Shakespeare—"I'm not male or female either but…," "Stoned men think they are different from stoned women…," "I want manly things and should not, women come to me," etc. Just as Shakespeare's "friend" inspired many of his sonnets, in Mayer's book the homoerotic figure of "Grace"—as well as other paramours—functions as Muse. (The classical Graces, praised by Pindar, were thought to *be* Muses.) The poems for Grace, "hypnopompic verges of the sublime," are beautiful, and, like most of the poems in the book, frankly or implicitly erotic without crossing the line into either the violently pornographic or sappy sweet. Again, like Shakespeare, Mayer's poems are wise and ephiphanic observations on the "immortal fear of love" where "Everyone makes love to their bereft & go."

Borrowing David C. D. Gansz's notion of "sin tactics," which raises both sexual and linguistic strategies, it is worth pausing to make a few observations regarding syntax in these sonnets. Mayer's "speaking without / stopping," an age-old, sometimes derogatory attribute of women's language, produces startling enjambment, such as the following octave:

> *Many times by a poet who saw you female of art*
> *The wish to make you lost began & can't say that*
> *That to be so old again as identified father*
> *Ignorant Orion was said to settle the bill mom*
> *Like settles stand for all night gives but without*
> *You feel another whose vagina somewhat over love her*
> *Communicating mother in fidelity I am thus plus*
> *Which I thought still but without sphere her here*

Certainly this passage is rife with puns, such as "bill" which recalls Bill "The Bard" Shakespeare (whose lexicon also testifies to a fascination with stars), or the "in fidelity" which is both a loyalty and a betrayal. If the refusal of linearity and closure is a property of women's writing (see essays by Lyn Hejinian and Beverly Dahlen in *Poetics Journal* 4), then the built-in resistance of Mayer's lines—their sinful refusal to assume singular meaning—is tantamount to a gender-challenge in the text.

To take this idea even one risky step further, the 'openness' of women's writing, as Luce Irigaray has suggested, accords with biologic fact—women open, men insert. Another prolific sonneteer, Ted Berrigan, for very different reasons, called the sonnet a "box"; in some peculiar way, it is vaginal: the reader 'enters' the sonnet, ostensibly for that pleasure, enjoying, as Mayer says in her maternal note, "the dilation of a form like the unbelievability and consequent common acceptance of the something of giving birth…," which recalls lines already quoted, "the rhyme / Of the jewel you pay attention to becomes you baby born." Writing and reading are, in other words, procreative acts: the writer creates writing; the reader creates a reading.

One 'generative' element is syntax, according to linguist Noam Chomsky. In what I can only describe (for lack of adequate vocabulary) as 'looping' word order ("the circular casements in which we're about") with repeated elements (word, phrase, syllable, phoneme), Mayer achieves a textual opacity which, somehow, avoids taking itself *too* seriously; even in the possibly tragic context of poverty and angst, Mayer embeds a zesty giggle. The romping syntax of her line is, at times, astonishing; she avoids the trap of syntactic homogeneity through modulation of syntactic orders, contrasting 'normative' units with 'strange' ones as she does in the following sestet –

> *Absence like parents is the astrophysical*
> *What who knows come in I've got my birth control out*
> *Come by get lost the curtain if fictionally red is not then*
> *real*
> *Nor's the blood shed why for what, we warn television*
> *of it*
> *Don't say anything bad like fuck or shit or otherwise*
> *and besides*
> *You might have to wear ostensible clothing & hairdos*
> *all your life*

—where the last two lines (with their relatively light *ostranenie*) are *almost* reassuringly familiar. Moreover, the imperative "Don't say anything bad like fuck or shit" is indicative of another pattern in Mayer's *Sonnets* in which poems seemingly address the poet and/or each other. Many punning couplets indulge in self-referential humor, such as "Sex, where's the couplet?" while others suggest the poet's affection for the form, "Couplet I adore you its my habit." But in the best Shakespearean tradition, the poet has doubts. In the "Note," Mayer writes:

> *How serious notorious and public a form, to think you could find the solution to a problem or an ending to an observation in one brief moment—a fraction of an abreaction of the science of the pattern of crumbs appearing on the table from the eating of a loaf of bread. Why are we as human beings so sturdy? How can we conscion existence much less love? Is that why we have philosophy? Why deconstruct so innately? Is the sonnet form a form of abdication from reality? Because it is so neat & thus does have conclusion? Is poetry's method of conclusion disjoined to for instance the life of the bee? If there are no conclusions why do we wish for them?*

The poet's doubt in the form has led her to discover it anew. If it was possible for a poet like Sydney or Surrey or Shakespeare to isolate an experience and process it in 14 lines, with the full confidence of Renaissance humanist ideology backing his attempt, then in the apocalyptic, contradictory world of postmodern fragmentation and inclusion, such an undertaking seems artificial, even absurdly anachronistic. Today's sonnets do not carry the same assumptions as sonnets written four hundred and fifty years ago. The prevalence of a form—or its idiosyncrasy—is, of course, coterminous with the age in which that form is proposed. In her new book,

Mayer has

> *...countered the concept of sonnet not with its meters*
> *The way thought proceeds countable like geologic stuff*
>   *is not;*
> *Not not countable's the specificity of love*
> *Couplet opposites yes of streams of no...*

Notice that negation runs through this passage: "four not(s)" (three of them adjacent), one "no," one "counter," and two implicit "counters" in the two "countable(s)," which reminds me of Barrett Watten's contempt of "negation" and resistance which he finds so central to the current literary milieu (see "XYZ of Reading" in *Conduit*). What is being negated here is the 'establishment' morés, expectations, boundaries, codes— to which Mayer opposes the renegade "specificity" of "love."

> *This is my new form of the sonnet*
> *This is the closing of it*
> *Please don't stop loving me right this moment*
> *Or else one of us might kill the other*
> *Just like in the papers*

Clearly I've just begun to indicate a few possible readings of this marvelous book. If I had time and space, I might undertake "The Trope of the Automobile in Mayer's *Sonnets*" or "*Corpus Interuptus* and *In Media Res* in Mayer's *Sonnets*" or "Architecture and Food in Mayer's *Sonnets*" or "The 'Trace' of *Memory* & *Utopia* in Mayer's *Sonnets*" or even "Beat Poet, New York Poet, or Language Poet: Mayer's *Sonnets*." This is the problem of a review as the provisional form and also its blessing. I've read the book. Now it's your turn.

In a poem, list what you know.

Address a poem to the reader.

Write household poems - about cooking, shopping, eating and
sleeping.
Write dream collaborations in the lune form.

Write poems that only make use of the words included in
Basic English.

Attempt to write about jobs and how they affect the writing
of poetry.

Write while being read to from science texts,

Trade poems with others and do not consider them your own.

Exercises in style: Write twenty-five or more different versions
of one event.

Review the statement: "What is happening to me, allowing for lies
and exaggerations which I try to avoid, goes into my poems."

Please add to this list.

Also, hypnagogic (the state between waking
+ sleeping)-work with both words
and visions.
        (hypnopompic (state
between sleeping +
        waking))